T0198864

Uniquely Peculiar
1 Peter 2:9

My Life Thru Poetry

Paulette Geddes

authorHOUSE®

AuthorHouse™
1663 Liberty Drive
Bloomington, IN 47403
www.authorhouse.com
Phone: 1 (800) 839-8640

Published by AuthorHouse 10/08/2018

ISBN: 978-1-5462-4088-4 (sc)
ISBN: 978-1-5462-4087-7 (e)

Library of Congress Control Number: 2018905307

Print information available on the last page.

ACKNOWLEDGEMENT

❖ A special thanks to my children, Preston Harden & Phillip Loken.

❖ To all my relatives, friends, Malaby's Crossroads Missionary Baptist Church (Knightdale, NC) and others who have assisted me along this journey sharing their support, either financially, morally, physically and spiritually, I say thank you.

❖ Most of all, I thank and praise God for giving me His grace and mercy through it all.

CONTENTS

INTRODUCTION

Are you "uniquely peculiar?

Do you consider yourself alone, an outcast, "in the world, but not of the world", On the outside looking in? Wondering why? Are you different in some aspect from most of the people you associate with?

Do you sense a greater need for something that is lacking in your life?

If you answered yes to any of the above questions, we share a common bond of Christian faith and historical consequences.

This bond dates back to "in the beginning". 1 Peter 2:9, "But ye are a chosen generation, a royal priesthood, a holy nation, a peculiar people; that ye should shew forth the praises of him who hath called you out of darkness into his marvellous light;".

Peculiar is derived from the Latin *peculium*, and denotes, as rendered in the RSV (a people for God's own possession"; a special possession or property.

Yes, I am uniquely peculiar, I know this now At first, I was timid and shy, but now God has inspired me to share my life through this collection of verses which details many aspects of my life, past and present. Some won't be pretty, as you know, but it IS my life.

As you read the pages, you will be able to see my transformation into a "uniquely peculiar" person. You may see yourself as well.

GUIDANCE

OUR PARENTS

They protect us from all danger
They tell us when we're wrong
They're always trying to help us
To lead us from all harm

They are the seeds of kindness
The Rose of everlasting Love
The sweetest fruit of gratitude
Our gift from above

They tell us what we need
Because the road is long and hard
They say, we need their guidance
But, most of all, Faith in God

We will always remember their sayings
And the things they helped us to do
And all this poem is really saying is
Parents, we love you!

MOTHER

Who is loving, sweet and kind
Who fills your every need
The one you'll always find
The one you'll always please

Who picks you up when you fall
To help you along each day
Who's a friend to all
And guides you each step of the way

Who is she?
Think a moment and another
To realize that
She's your Mother.

MOTHER'S BIRTHDAY

Your day comes but once a year
So Happy Birthday Mother dear

Our present to you is from heaven above
A gift to our Mother, the gift of Love

We love you to the bottoms of our hearts
Always hoping that we shall never part

We love you very much, dear Mother of ours
We hope that your love for us will never grow sour

From all of your children, we have this to say,
To a very nice person, Happy Birthday.

THE IMPORTANCE OF A MOTHER

The most important person in my life
Is my Mother. She means more than a
Father, sister or brother.

She is a housekeeper, babysitter,
And wife, but most of all she is the
Only person that can give life.

God made her powerful than anyone else
On earth. Because anyone can take a life,
But only a Mother can give birth.

SCHOOL IS IN

The buses come
And school is in
The bell rings
Then class begins

The teacher gets a book
And begins to call the roll
She sees a student chewing gum
So out the student goes

The dean goes to the restroom
And to her surprise, she smells smoke
Then the students are sent home
To their parents with a suspension note!

The end of the school day is here
And the teachers and students are glad
Then the teacher says "test tomorrow"
Now, this makes the students mad!

So bring some paper
And a pencil and pen
Then study like crazy
because school is in.

WE WRITE

We write right or write wrong
We write how we feel, we do it alone

We write using our senses
We write without pretenses

We write freely, rhythm, or rhyme
Using meter or we write in time

We write right or we write wrong
writing, this is where we belong

LIFE BATTLES

KEEPING SILENT IS....

The enemy of the people
The aftermath of "who cares"
The speechless activist
The friend of the opposition
The rewards of nothing will happen
The subliminal racism
The enemy of the revolution

The muted tongue
The fall of democracy
The voice of nobody
The outspoken nonvoter
The mouth of the faceless
The myth of "it will eventually work out"
The motionless movement

The going up on the down escalator
The eyes of reality
The cry of "that's the way it's always been"
The "hushed" victim
The continual unchanging
The "see something, say nothing"
The unconscious agreement
The repetition of life

Keeping Silent.

A PECULIAR PERSON

In the World, but not of the World

I thought I was a righteous person
Because I didn't drink, smoke or dance
But other sins had me falling
Deeper into the devil's hand

Now I can see what's going on
Because the devil is all around
But I know with God's help
The devil can be bound

People look at me and say
I look different and don't fit in
However, I know Christ had cleansed me
And took away my sins

Strange at it may sound to others
And peculiar as I may seem to be
I believe and trust in God and that
Heaven is waiting for me

In the world, but not of the world
Is sometimes trying to me, but I know
I can do all things through Christ,
Who strengthens me.

THE BATTLE

I was a sin-sick sinner
No contentment did I know
But one day Jesus came
To save my very soul

Now the devil was awatching
He tried to steal my joy
But with the armor of the Lord
The devil will be destroyed

Some days he had me doubting
Some days I even sinned
But through God's grace and repentance
This battle I'm able to win

The war is never over
The battle is always raging
But Jesus is my fortress
And I'll forever stand

THE WORLD AND ITS PROBLEMS

Why is there hate
On this planet called earth
What does a baby really
Get into on his day of birth

Why are there Wars
Poverty and Pollution
Why can't we find
One simple solution

People killing each other
For something or another
Why can't there be peace
And loving sisters and brothers

WHAT??

How did it happen
I wasn't expecting it
What did I do
To deserve it

It wasn't my fault
I wasn't even there
You don't know me.
I don't care

You don't understand
Why it was so
So leave me along
And just go

MASSACRE

Another school shooting

Mom and dads panicking

Ammunitions, guns, and rifles

Students running for their lives

Security and safety null and void

Another senseless shooting

Children scared and crying

Ricocheting magazine bullets

Endless blood everywhere

IS THIS A DREAM

Is this a dream
Is this really going on
Please awaken me
I've been sleeping too long

Tell me what has happened
To our love for each other
Why all this hatred
Against one another

I see government officials lying
And the little children crying
People dying, fighting and killing
People lying. people stealing

Dream or reality
There has to be a way
We can't go on living
With this happening every day

COLOR BORN

MY BIG BROTHER

My big brother
Is just like me, Black and
Beautiful and wants to be free

My big brother is a bundle
Of joy, but he gets mad when
You call him "boy"

My big brother went to ride on
The bus, he had to sit to the
Back to avoid a fuss

My big brother joined the marines
To fight for the country that
Treated him mean

My big brother laughed until he
Cried, that was the day,
My big brother died

My big brother is Black
Like me, but now my big
Brother is truly free.

COLOR BORN NOT COLOR BLIND

I was born into this color
A choice not of my own
A family trait for me to wear
A color that we share

We all share the colors
of skin tone degrees
But that shouldn't determine
How you treat me

Color born doesn't dictate my life
Or me having a peace of mind,
Color born only shows me
That you're not color blind

WHO AM I

Am I the child of my father and mother
Or am I
The sister to my sisters and brothers

Am I the cause of the white man's bigotry
Or am I
A burden to the black man's dignity

Am I the reflected image from a painted glass
Or am I
An accident from my mother's past

Am I the new savior of my world
Or am I
Just a plain poor black girl

Who am I

LOVE

WHERE IS LOVE

Where is love
Love is all around
But just you wait
And love will come in time

Love is everywhere
In houses, schools
In churches, in stores,
And even behind locked doors

Love is everywhere
Love is all around
But just you wait
And love will come in time.

WILL YOU BE MINE

When I look up at night
And see the shining stars
I think about you, what
You're doing, where you are

When I'm away from you.
I think of you very much
I want to be with you, and
Feel the gentleness of your touch

I wanted to ask you this
But it wasn't the right time
So, it's now or never
Please, will you be mine?

TWO TIMER

Last night you told me
I was the only girl for you
Today, I heard you telling
Another girl the same thing too

I gave myself to you, and
Would have given you the world
Now you tell me to go away
Because you've found another girl

You seemed to be
So sincere and kind
While all the time
You had someone else in mind

Everyone said that we made a good couple
But they just couldn't see
That while I was loving you.
You were two-timing me

I know now that love is blind
But now that I can see
I see what a fool I've been
And that you were no good for me

THE WEDDING

Here comes the bride, the organist begins to play
As the bride walks out her mother begins to cry
Because her daughter is being given away

While the minister is praying
The bride looks backwards into the past
She remembers the words, only true love will last

When she met him, the darkness became light
Because somehow both knew
It was love, love at first sight

Now she's going to be a wife
To a man who loves her and she'll
Love him for the rest of their life

She won't ever forget the way
He looked at her and said "I do"
For that was their wedding day.

SHORT VERSES

THE WALK

White
Wedding dress pure, walking down the aisle
slipped on a rose petal, everything went
Black

FORGETTING THE THOUGHT

A while ago, I had it
But I forgot it,
Considering it probably wasn't that important
Did it slip my mind?
Oh well, it will come back to me.

ANXIOUS

Desperate
Edgy
Fumbling here and there
Grasping at straws
Anxious

RAIN

Small little droplets
Falling loudly on the roof
Trying to seep through

PEOPLE

They are born and they
Are educated and after they
Have died, they become appreciated

DEATH: THE SALVATION FROM SUFFERING

A baby was born dead yesterday. Nobody knew why.
The mother was in perfect health. So why did the baby die?

DEAD

Desolate body on the ground
Endless blood forever flowing
All the world is quiet and still
Death is knocking at your windowsill

SAD

Sitting along by myself, mad and sad
At the world and myself
Doing nothing but crying all day

FAITH

MY GOD

My God is Good
He feeds the hungry
When they have no food

My God is True
He doesn't try to act
Against me and you

My God is Love
He loves everyone
Sister, brother, mother, and dad

My God is Dependable
Whenever you call him,
He will always answer

My God is Powerful
For who else could fix the
Sun to shine all over this world

My God is Great
For who else could create
A world in six days!

SIN

Hello there, my name is Sin
I'm going to tell you a story
Don't be afraid come on in

I was born in a place
Where souls are put up for sale
A place well known, a place called Hell

I am in your world to see you cry,
To see you fight, steal, kill and
Then to see you die

I cause things like
Prejudices, pollution
Wars and revolutions

Now you have heard my story
So pick your place to dwell
A place called Heaven
Or be with me in Hell

I AM BUT A CHILD

What can I say
What can I do
Who will listen to me
Will you?

Will you listen when I tell you
How God saved me
And how my life has been
Changed since Jesus made me free

Other children listen and look
They can see Christ in me
But because I'm a child
You won't even hear me

I may not know or understand
Your problems, trials, and pains
But just because I am a child
Doesn't mean I can't complain

Sex, drugs, peer pressure
Alcohol, music, and TV
Are some of the things that Satan
Is using to try to destroy me

Yes, I am a child
Young in mind, young in age
But don't let it stop you from listening to me
For I have something to say

But because I am a child
Fearless, willing, ready to change
I see what God has done for me
And with you, He can do the same

Jesus came to me
Just like He did to you
I am a child, a child of the King
And I know He loves me too.

THROW THE BOOK AT ME

Throw the book at me
And with my outstretched hand
I will catch it and read it
And then I will understand

Throw the book at me
I won't pick it up, you see
Sometimes it's hard
to get on bended knee

Throw the book at me
So I can drop my troubles and pain
And catch the Word of God
So I can be born again

Throw the book at me
Oh, it may hurt a while,
Just when it touches my soul
It will cause me to smile

Please throw the book at me
I need it now, more than ever
To help me with life situations
To conquer Satan's endeavors

Please throw the book at me
That my memory it may jog
To remember my mothers' sayings
Have faith and believe in God

WHAT DID WE GET FOR CHRISTMAS

What did we get for Christmas, you all know the story
Of clothes too big or small, Of things we didn't need at all

What did I get for Christmas, I can't even remember it
Was it something that I needed, where is it? Did I lose it

The tie is the wrong color, The shoes don't fit
The bicycle parts are missing, The children won't keep quiet

The lines are too long. The traffic is a mess
The fact is we've forgotten the true meaning of Christmas

God so loved the world that He gave His only son
Now through Jesus Christ, our battles are already won

Christmas is a symbol of Christ coming to earth
To change filthy rags into spiritual worth

He came to save our souls from a world full of sin
All we have to do is to open our hearts and let Him in.

So let us rejoice and glorify His name
And don't forget the reason why Jesus Christ came

Our greatest present came from heaven above
The gift of salvation, The gift of Love

THE VISION

Sometimes I look into the mirror
And don't like what I see
But then a joy overwhelms me
Because I know Jesus loves me

People look at me and see a person
With faults and imperfections
But God looks at me and
Sees His greatest creation

The vision of ourselves is often
Filled with pretense, insecurity and pride
But Jesus views us as children of God
Walking by His side

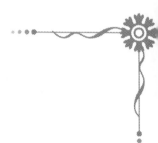

WHAT DOES LOVE HAVE TO DO WITH IT?

Jesus says, if you love me, keep my commandments, (John 14:15)

I told the Lord I love Him, He said that He could hear it
But through all the talking that I had done, the love, he could not see it

The super bowl, or the TV show or the car being cleansed on Sunday. I'll go to church when I'm done or I'll try and to press my way

I've never harmed a single soul with hands, knife or gun
But can I say I never hurt anyone with the movement of my tongue?

I had to tell the first lie to keep the truth from sounding so cold
Now there are so many lies, I don't know which ones I've told

He said he would not force me, it was my decision, he said
We were engaged to be married, so we had sex anyway

They said there were trying to protect me, when they told me not to stay out all night. Just because they got in trouble when they were young, don't' mean they're always right.

They say the Lord is blessing, a new home, a new car, plasma TV. Well, I'm doing everything at church, where is the blessing for me?

That driver cut in front of me, trying to make me late for church,
driving in the wrong lane. That word just slipped out, I didn't
mean to take His name in vain.

Yes, Lord, I love you, not my future you see?
Depart from me, He said, you worker of iniquity

What does love have to do with it?

Jesus says, if you love me, keep my commandments

WOMEN CALLED TO DO EXTRAORDINARY THINGS

We are called by God to do extraordinary things
From the beginning of time, His path was made plain

Eve started it, Sarah had hope
Rahab was redeemed, and Ruth was loved

Deborah was judge, Hannah was graceful
Abigail was honest, Esther had faith

Mary was blessed, the Samaritan woman was thirsty
Martha was working, her sister Mary was worshipping

Mary Magdalene was delivered, Lydia was a businesswoman
Esther was courageous, and Jael was strong

Women called to do extraordinary things
They are gone, but the issues remain

Our past cannot quiet us, our present cannot defeat us
Our future is before us, His calling is in us.

Our plan is clear and our purpose is unchanged
we are women, called to do extraordinary things

ARE YOU A CHRISTIAN?

Are you a Christian? Have you grown in your walk?
Are you there yet? Or do you just talk the Talk

Are you mature in your faith? Do you talk more than you listen?
Is your faith just a coat of paint, a gloss, never glistening

1 Peter 2:2 talks about babes who desire the sincere milk of the word
Has it grown sour and overtime, turned into curds?

Are you a Christian? Are you saved?
Is it something that you believe or is it how you behave?

Are you a Christian? Are you Christ-like?
Do you put it on the altar? Or do you start the fight?

Ok, you say you are a Christian? I can't confirm or deny
But your actions seem contrary, Don't make me have to lie

Are you a Christian? A Christian down to the bone
It's not a title you wear, It's a title you own.

Are you a Christian?

THE CHAIR...BLIND FAITH

Just bend my body down and sit
I never look to see if its legs will split

Will it contain my weight
Or will the floor be my fate

Is it strong and sturdy for my pounds
Or will it give way to the ground

I never wonder about its hold
I just sit proudly and bold

STORIES

THE POWER OF THREE:
Me, Myself, and I

Me, Myself, and I were triplets, living together to make ends meet. Me was self-centered always wanting the main focus; "It's all about <u>me</u>" Myself was conservative and independent; "I can do it <u>myself</u>". I was the domineering one, wanting to have things I's way because; "<u>I</u> said so"

But every now and then, Me would give in, Myself would ask for help and I would come down to earth a little. Sometimes you could even hear Me, Myself, and I arguing. Unfortunately nothing was done until Me, Myself, and I worked together, the power of three.

The Twins: Goodness & Kindness

Goodness was a quiet person, Kindness was full of energy. They were twins. Most people couldn't tell them apart. Both had the same "ness" about them. Both saw the positive side in everything and everybody. Goodness always believes that doing the right thing was the right thing. She was, for the most part, a well-behaved child, as most of our children are. Kindness believed that on acting on the right thing toward others was the right thing to do. Kindness was a friendly and warm-hearted person. Goodness and Kindness had very caring parents. Their mother, Grace, who always taught them about Charity, is generous and helpful. She told them about the undeserved favor of God. Their father, Mercy was a powerful man in his own right. He was a humble and forgiving person.

One day while walking in the field, Goodness and Kindness saw a rabbit eating the crops. They ran after the rabbit to scare him away. While running away, the rabbit got caught in a bear trap. It was out of the range that their mother told them not to go. Goodness says "we shouldn't go any further". However Kindness couldn't bear seeing the rabbit stuck in the trap, trying to escape and bleeding. She begged to Goodness, "I know we are not supposed to go out of the fence, but the rabbit is hurt". Goodness thought about it, she knew if she went outside the gate, she would be disobeying her parents.

If she did not go, the rabbit would die and she did not want to think about that. "OK", she said. Kindness was excited. Goodness and Kindness ran toward the rabbit. They realized their running toward him frightened him, and he would try to hurt himself getting out of the trap. They slowly came upon him and together with Goodness and Kindness; he was freed from the trap. They smiled at each other.

They had done a good and kind deed and could get back to the fence without their parents ever knowing. But then, the rabbit was crawling, barely moving across the field. Their caring for this rabbit made them realized that it needed some first aid. Goodness mentioned that bringing the rabbit back to the house would let their parents know for sure that they went outside the gate. Kindness said that they must take the chance for the sake of the animal. Goodness took off her jacket and with kindness wrapped the rabbit in the jacket and picked him up and walked carefully to the house, not knowing how their parents would take it.

Grace was preparing the evening dinner when she heard a noise from outside. "Mom, Mom", Kindness screamed. Grace came running to the kitchen screen door to see what was happening. Goodness and Kindness had the rabbit on the porch, both were crying. "Mama, he's hurt, what can we do?" Grace got some bandages and ointment while she told Goodness to call the local vet. The vet lived nearby, so he came right away. The animal was fixed up and going to stay at the vet until he was able to hop again.

By that time, Goodness was very worried about the "going outside of the fence, thing" and so was Kindness. Grace told them that "as soon as Mercy gets home, we will discuss what you did together". The children went back to studying and playing in their rooms, waiting on their father.

As Mercy, arrived home, the children greeted him as always, however this time they were crying. He knew that something was wrong. They, almost together told him what had happened. After hearing their story, Mercy had to talk with Grace. After Grace and Mercy got together, they knew what had to be done. Mercy called Goodness and Kindness. Goodness and Kindness came in the room slowly together as close as twins could possibly be.

Grace gave them favor and Mercy showed forgiveness. Grace talked about how nice and helpful the children were to the animal, even though it could get them into trouble. Now the children awaited Mercy, He was a big man, even while sitting down. He saw them through the eyes of forgiveness. He told them that because they tried to help a hurting animal, even knowing that they would get in trouble for it, that they sacrificed themselves for the sake of another, Mercy forgave them. You see, Goodness and Kindness go together hand in hand. Grace protects us and Mercy forgives us. Mercy sat Goodness and Kindness on his knees and began to tell them the story about Love. Love was their neighbor.

To be continued…

Printed in the United States
By Bookmasters